*writing guides*

ACTIVITIES FOR WRITING

# Persuasive
# WRITING

JILLIAN POWELL

C000281443

# CONTENTS

# INTRODUCTION

The Scholastic *Writing Guides* series provides teachers with ideas and projects that promote a range of writing, bringing insights from educational research into the classroom. Each guide explores a different type of writing and provides example material, background information, photocopiable activities and teaching suggestions. Their aim is to enable teachers to guide the writing process, share planning ideas and develop themes as a context for writing activities.

The materials:
- motivate children with interesting activities
- break complex types of writing into manageable teaching units
- focus on and develop the typical features of particular types of writing
- provide original approaches to teaching.

Each book is divided into sections, beginning with examples of the type of writing being taught. These are followed by ideas for developing writing and projects that will extend over a series of sessions.

## SECTION ONE: USING GOOD EXAMPLES

Section One looks at good examples of the genre, with the emphasis on using texts to stimulate and develop writing. Two example texts are shared, and questions that focus the discussion on their significant features are suggested. This is followed by activities that explore what the texts can teach us about writing, enabling teachers to compare the two texts and to go on to model the type of writing presented in the guide.

## SECTION TWO: DEVELOPING WRITING

Section Two moves from reading to writing. This section provides activities that prompt and support children in planning and writing. A range of approaches includes planning templates and strategies to stimulate ideas. The activities refine children's ideas about the type of writing being developed and give them focused writing practice in the context of scaffolded tasks. Teacher's notes support each activity by explaining the objective and giving guidance on delivery.

## SECTION THREE: WRITING

Section Three moves on to writing projects. Building upon the earlier work in Section Two, these projects aim to develop the quality of writing and provide a selection of ideas for class or group work on a particular theme or idea. The teacher may choose to use some or all of the ideas presented in each project as a way of weaving the strategies developed in Section Two into a more complex and extended writing task.

## SECTION FOUR: REVIEW

Section Four supports the assessment process. Children are encouraged to reflect on the type of writing they are tackling and to evaluate how effectively their work has met the criteria for the genre identified in Section One.

# Earthquake!

## Oxfam Appeal
# INDIA
## Earthquake

**Your money is needed now.**

Oxfam has been working with local partners in Gujarat, India, since 1977. As news of the earthquake came through, Oxfam's Emergency Team flew out to join them. They urgently need your help.

Several hundred thousand people are homeless, cold, hungry, thirsty, and shocked. Your money could help pay for clean water, blankets, shelters, food, and health care.

Your money will also be vital in the coming months as Oxfam works with families to rebuild homes, livelihoods, and villages.

**Help today by phoning**

# 01865 313131

**Or donate online: www.oxfam.org.uk**

**Or send your gift with the coupon below to:**

**Oxfam INDIA EARTHQUAKE Appeal**

**Oxfam, Room BBA002, Freepost, Oxford OX2 7BR**

**Yes, I will help. Here is my gift of:**

£25 ☐    £50 ☐    £100 ☐    £250 ☐    £ _____

Mr, Mrs, Miss, Ms _____

Address _____

_____

_____ Postcode _____

**Please send to:** Oxfam, Room BBA002, Freepost, Oxford OX2 7BR

Tick here if you don't want your details shared with like-minded charities ☐

### Oxfam

# Save Scroby Sands

Dear Sir,

I am writing to oppose plans for a wind farm on Scroby Sands. It is outrageous to think about putting wind turbines on the sandbanks, in full view of the seafront and beach at Great Yarmouth.

The whole reason for sitting on the seafront or the beach and looking out to sea is to spend time relaxing away from everything artificial and to enjoy looking at the natural world for a change. Who wants to look at ugly wind turbines which, unlike ships, are always there?

Nature organisations have already expressed concern about the wildlife which uses this habitat, including terns, seals and birds of migration. One of the most enjoyable trips at Yarmouth is in the little boat to Scroby Sands to see the seals in their natural surroundings – not to visit a wind farm!

There are few enough natural places left these days and Scroby Sands is far too precious to become a 'power station'. I believe the wind power companies are only interested in profit. A wind farm always depends on the weather. It can only produce a small amount of power, yet it will spoil the environment forever. Let us hope that somebody in authority will come to their senses before it is too late and stop the destruction of these beautiful sandbanks.

Yours faithfully,

Pat Doddington

*Children will be familiar with many forms of the persuasive genre, such as advertisements, slogans, school brochures, sales leaflets, and letters and editorials in comics and magazines. Persuasive texts set out to convince the reader of something. They enlist facts and opinions to construct a logical argument made up of strong statements, as well as using techniques such as catchy slogans, alliteration and humour, positive language, rhetorical questions, emphasis and exaggeration. Knowledge of the genre will help children to set out an argument clearly, write logical sentences, and understand how emotive language can be used to evoke a response in their readers.*

## Shared activities

### Earthquake!

Photocopiable page 4 is part of an Oxfam appeal launched after the earthquake in Gujarat, India in January 2001. Read the text with the children, going over any difficult vocabulary. Point out that it is in the form of an advertisement. Ask them what most adverts persuade us to do: buy something. An appeal is different because it is asking us to spend money to help others. Does the advert make the children feel they could make a difference and help these people? Would it persuade them to send a donation? Explore the format of the text in more detail, looking at key features of the genre, for example the big, bold *INDIA* to catch people's attention (explain that this event was in the news a lot at the time); a short, dramatic opening statement (also in bold) supported by, in this case, quite a shocking fact – *Several hundred thousand people*; the use of powerful, emotive language, such as *now, urgently, vital*.

### Save Scroby Sands

Photocopiable page 5 is an example of a letter written to a local newspaper opposing the proposal for a wind farm on Scroby Sands, a sandbank formation three kilometres off the coastline of Great Yarmouth in Norfolk. This project for the largest offshore wind farm in the UK provoked strong feelings, for and against, among locals.

After reading the letter with the children, explain that wind power is a renewable energy source that can provide electricity without contributing to pollution (apart from noise) or global warming. Wind turbines provide a cheap and clean form of power, so why is the writer of the letter opposed to the wind farm? Find language that reveals the depth of her feelings and attempts to persuade others to her point of view, such as *outrageous, ugly, far too precious, destruction*. Go through the structure of the letter. Point out the strong opening statement; the presentation of argument supported by details, including assumption of agreement (*The whole reason for…, One of the most enjoyable trips…*) and the summary tying points together. Do the children agree with the writer or take another view?

### SOS!

Display the 'Earthquake!' advertisement and go through the questions on photocopiable page 8 in detail as you discuss it. What facts are we told about Gujarat? Ask the children what they think it tells us about people's lives in this part of India, knowing that Oxfam has been working there for over 20 years. What is the situation there after the earthquake? Demonstrate how the advert uses repetition to get a point across, for example all the words that convey urgency and crisis. Ask the children to count how many times the phrase *your money* or *your help* is repeated. Look at the length of the sentences in the advert. Which are kept very short and snappy to emphasise the message? (The opening statement and closing *Help today…*)

**Soapbox**

Display the letter on photocopiable page 5. Remind the children that the writer is expressing a strong point of view. She is opposed to the wind farm and is trying to persuade the newspaper readers (and the local planning authority) that she is right. The wind power company and its supporters will take another point of view. Together, read some of the facts about the proposed wind farm on photocopiable page 9 and consider the letter-writer's opinion on each of these facts, based on her letter. For example, on the point that the wind farm will help the environment, she will counter that it is damaging the environment by spoiling a lovely, natural view. On the point that the wind farm will provide electricity for thousands of homes, she will argue that it has to rely on the weather and can only provide a small amount of electricity. Complete the activity together, using the children's suggestions.

# Taking ideas further

**Persuasion**

This activity invites the children to compare the two samples of persuasive writing. The questions highlight genre features shared by the two texts. They ask the children to consider what the texts are trying to achieve (and how), and to look closely at vocabulary and textual devices used to persuade the reader. They also invite children to start thinking creatively from a persuasive point of view, by suggesting picture briefs and slogans which could support each text.

**Persuade**

Photocopiable page 11 uses the form of a washing powder advertisement to draw together key features of persuasive texts that the children have come across so far, as well as suggesting other techniques that they will be using in Section Two activities. It can be enlarged as a classroom poster and used for reference when the children are discussing or writing persuasive texts.

**Extension ideas**

● Encourage children to become more familiar with the persuasive genre by noting other examples. These can include printed advertisements and those on radio and television; glossy travel brochures; estate agents' details; classified ads; sales leaflets and cards; health promotion pamphlets, such as those persuading children against tobacco and other drugs. As well as collecting examples, the children could write brief reviews of adverts they have seen or heard.
● Spend a shared session exploring which adverts the children find most persuasive and why. Ask them to bring in examples of adverts they like, and pass them round so the class can give their opinions of how well they work.
● If the children have been studying the Second World War in history lessons, they can look at examples of war-time propaganda, such as posters and leaflets encouraging people to 'dig for victory', save water or follow the rules of the black-out.
● Collect cuttings about any controversial local issues, such as the building of a bypass, traffic calming measures for a dangerous road or the closure of a school. These can be used to start a class discussion on how to get across a persuasive point of view. What can the children suggest could be done to support the cause? (For example, writing letters to the local newspaper, organising a march with banners, making posters to display locally.)

# SOS!

Read each of these questions and look in the advert for the word or phrase that answers it. Circle the word or phrase and draw a line to link it back to its question.

**Who has Oxfam sent out?**

**What problems are the local people having?**

**How many people are in need?**

**Whose help is needed?**

**How can you give money?**

**Where did the earthquake happen?**

**How soon is help needed?**

**What will donations help to pay for now?**

**How will any money given now help in the future?**

## Oxfam Appeal INDIA Earthquake

**Your money is needed now.**

Oxfam has been working with local partners in Gujarat, India, since 1977. As news of the earthquake came through, Oxfam's Emergency Team flew out to join them. They urgently need your help.

Several hundred thousand people are homeless, cold, hungry, thirsty, and shocked. Your money could help pay for clean water, blankets, shelters, food, and health care.

Your money will also be vital in the coming months as Oxfam works with families to rebuild homes, livelihoods, and villages.

Help today by phoning
**01865 313131**

Or donate online: www.oxfam.org.uk
Or send your gift with the coupon below to:
Oxfam INDIA EARTHQUAKE Appeal
Oxfam, Room BBA002, Freepost, Oxford OX2 7BR

Yes, I will help. Here is my gift of:
£25 ☐    £50 ☐    £100 ☐    £250 ☐    £ _____

Mr, Mrs, Miss, Ms _____

Address _____

_____

_____ Postcode _____

**Please send to:** Oxfam, Room BBA002, Freepost, Oxford OX2 7BR
Tick here if you don't want your details shared with like-minded charities ☐

**Oxfam**

Oxfam GB is a member of Oxfam International
Registered charity no 202918

# Soapbox

A letter can put across a point of view and try to persuade others to that point of view. What is the letter-writer's opinion on these points?

The turbines will be in view of Yarmouth Central Beach. _____
_____

_____

The wind farm will cost £75 million. _____

_____

_____

The area is famous for its wildlife, including seals and rare sea birds.

_____

_____

The wind farm will supply electricity to 52 000 homes. _____

_____

_____

The turbines will be 60 metres high. _____

_____

_____

The wind farm will provide employment for people in the local area.

_____

_____

The wind farm will provide clean energy and help the environment.

_____

_____

# Persuasion

Compare the two pieces of persuasive writing you have looked at so far.

|  | Earthquake! | Save Scroby Sands |
|---|---|---|
| What form is the text in? | | |
| What does the text aim to persuade the reader to do? | | |
| How does it appeal to the reader's feelings? | | |
| List three persuasive words used. | | |
| Find a fact that supports the argument. | | |
| Write a slogan to promote the campaign. | | |
| Suggest a brief for a picture that might help the campaign. | | |

*writing guides:* PERSUASIVE WRITING

**New improved**

**Our most persuasive formula yet!**

*Persuade*

washes arguments clean away

- Present tense
- Clear opening statement
- A closing summary
- Strong, positive language
- Opinions supported by evidence or reasons
- Reasonable tone
- Short, straightforward sentences
- Humour or other way of relating to the readers to win them over
- Alliteration, rhythm or rhyme for catchy, memorable slogans
- Connective words making logical links
- Question inviting agreement

TRY ME NOW!

# SECTION TWO

## DEVELOPING WRITING

*The activities in this section are designed to help children to gain a greater understanding of the generic features of persuasive writing. Each activity focuses on one aspect of the genre, such as structure, persuasive language or the use of fact and opinion. The activities also introduce different forms of persuasive writing, such as editorials, advertisements, letters and leaflets. They involve some class work and discussion, and some work individually or in pairs on the photocopiable sheets. This will generate topics and ideas for their own persuasive texts and develop skills that will be used in Section Three to write sustained pieces of persuasive writing.*

**OBJECTIVE**

■ To structure a persuasive text effectively.

## STATE YOUR CASE

### WHAT YOU NEED

Photocopiable page 16, scissors, glue, board or flip chart.

### WHAT TO DO

Remind the children that the texts they looked at in Section One had a clear structure. Demonstrate that a persuasive text begins with a statement setting out the argument, then supports that statement with evidence or reasons, before rounding off with a summary at the end. This activity will give the children practice in putting sentences in order to make an argument clear and persuasive.

Introduce the topic of global warming and ask the children if they know what it is. Use a simple diagram on the board to explain the principle that 'greenhouse' gases such as carbon dioxide from cars and industry are trapping heat from the Sun in the Earth's atmosphere and causing the Earth to warm up. Ask the children if they know any effects that this may have. (For example, the polar ice caps may melt, sea levels will rise, there will be more floods and droughts.)

Tell the children that they are going to arrange a series of sentences as a passage with the aim of persuading people to use their cars less often in order to reduce these greenhouse gases. Working in pairs or groups, they need to read through the sentences on the photocopiable sheet and decide how best to order them. The framework is marked out to help them organise the text. Advise the children to swap the sentences around and discuss them until the whole group is happy with the order, then paste them in place. Compare the results across the groups and assess how persuasive the piece is. The children can refer to this framework later, when organising their own material.

# GOOD CONNECTIONS

## WHAT YOU NEED

Photocopiable page 17, paper, scissors, glue, board or flip chart.

## WHAT TO DO

This activity focuses on persuasive writing at sentence and word level. Begin by introducing the topic of vegetarianism. Ask the children what they know about it. Are any of them vegetarian? Why do some people decide to be vegetarian? Write the children's suggestions on the board. Read the statements on photocopiable page 17 together. Remind the children that if they are trying to persuade someone to follow this diet, they will need to back up their argument with reasons why it is a good thing. On the sheet they will find facts which can be used to support each statement. They need to find two facts for each statement and position them before and/or after the statement. They should then link their sentences using different connective words. Remind the children that connectives are words or phrases that join sentences or parts of a sentence. Point out that when they are writing a persuasive text, connective words like these will provide useful links between their statements and the supporting evidence or examples, giving a cohesive logical argument that reads well.

### OBJECTIVES
■ To use connectives to help in structuring an argument.
■ To use connectives to link statements or opinions with evidence or reasons.

# WICKED CARS

## WHAT YOU NEED

Photocopiable page 18, paper, writing materials including coloured pencils, board or flip chart.

### OBJECTIVES
■ To learn how emotive language can manipulate the reader.
■ To consider the layout and format of a text.

## WHAT TO DO

Tell the children that they are going to think about the language ploys used in persuasive writing and the way words can be used to manipulate a reader's views. Write the word *cake* on the board. On either side of it write *delicious* and *fattening*. Both words can be used to describe cake. One makes it sound good, the other bad. Write the words *computer game* on the board and ask the children if they can think of any adjectives (or adjectival phrases) that would make it sound good or bad (*exciting, fun; boring* and so on).

Using the photocopiable sheet, apply this exercise to sports cars. Some of the words on the sheet make them sound good, others make them sound bad. The children can work in pairs to decide which words are positive and which negative, circling them in two different colours.

When they have done this, ask the children to work on their own sheets, using the two columns to organise the groups of words into *for* or *against*. Beside each adjective, they should write a few words to explain what each word tells us about fast cars – why it is a powerful word. For example, *dangerous* is negative, suggesting that fast cars can cause road accidents and injure or kill people.

The children can then use the material they have organised to prepare a leaflet arguing in favour of or against fast cars. They could use a sheet of folded A4 paper to make a leaflet, and begin thinking about layout and the impact of their text.

**OBJECTIVE**
■ To focus on persuasive language used for selling.

# TRY ME

## WHAT YOU NEED

Photocopiable page 19, writing materials, selection of product advertisements from comics, magazines or newspapers.

## WHAT TO DO

Ask the children to look at a selection of advertisements and choose the one that they think works best. Ask them to consider why it works. How is it persuasive? How does it appeal in just a few words? Why does it make them want to have that product? Discuss some of their findings, exploring ideas such as catchy names, snappy slogans, invented words, humour, rhyme, alliteration and so on.

Tell the children they are going to try thinking up names and slogans for four new products. They could also try to invent another product of their own to 'advertise'. For each product, they need to consider the information they are given and think about the buyers they want to appeal to – who is likely to buy the product and how can it be made to sound attractive? When they have completed the sheets, share the children's ideas for each product in turn, and discuss which names and slogans work best.

**OBJECTIVES**
■ To present a persuasive point of view.
■ To address and counter a point of view.

# VOX POP

## WHAT YOU NEED

Photocopiable page 20, writing materials, board or flip chart.

## WHAT TO DO

This activity investigates a range of opinions on the same subject, and helps children to address opposing points of view in their writing. Tell them that the sheet presents a range of views that people might have on computer games. Read out some of the quotes and start a discussion about the pros and cons of computer games. Ask the children how they would counter some of the arguments given, for example that computer games make people violent. They might suggest that it is easy to tell the difference between the fantasy of games and real life. Write some of their ideas on the board.

Now explain to the children that they are going to prepare ideas for a letter to a newspaper on the subject of computer games, but they should first decide which point of view they want to take. Are they going to praise computer games or criticise them? Advise that, once they have decided, they can write down their arguments and reasons in the box on the sheet. Encourage them to think about countering opposing views to make their persuasion stronger. Refer them to the letter on photocopiable page 5 to help them to set out their ideas.

**OBJECTIVES**
■ To distinguish between fact and opinion in a persuasive text.
■ To support or oppose an argument, giving reasons.

# POINTS OF VIEW

## WHAT YOU NEED

Photocopiable page 21, writing materials, board or flip chart.

## WHAT TO DO

Suggest to the children that both facts and opinions can be used as the basis for a persuasive text, but need backing up with evidence or reasons. To present a persuasive argument, the children need to have knowledge of their subject and give details to support their stance with reasons or evidence. Ask the children if they understand the difference between fact and opinion. Write some examples of both on the board.

For example *Getting a sun tan damages the skin* is a fact. No one can disagree with it because scientists have proved it. *A sun tan looks good* is an opinion. Some people may disagree with it; it is not an accepted truth.

Tell the children that they are going to look at each of the statements on the sheet and decide whether it is fact or opinion. Could it be backed up by factual details? Or is it just what someone thinks? If they think it is a fact, they should write a few words of evidence that support it. If they think it is just an opinion, they should say why they agree or disagree. For example, *Smoking is bad for you* – the statement is a fact; evidence could include *research has shown that smoking causes cancer and other diseases. Watching television is a waste of time* is an opinion. The children might agree and say it turns you into a couch potato, or disagree and suggest you can learn a lot from watching educational programmes, or simply that it is good fun.

# BE REASONABLE
## WHAT YOU NEED
Photocopiable page 22, writing materials.

## WHAT TO DO
Emphasise to the children that when they are writing a persuasive text, they need to consider who the text is aimed at. Who are they trying to convince and win over? Remind them that when they present a viewpoint, they will need to give reasons to support it. Ask the children to choose two of the topics on the sheet or include one of their own and state their opinion on that. They then need to write down three reasons for each topic that will add weight to their opinion and persuade the audience of its merits.

**OBJECTIVES**
■ To present an opinion and support it with reasons.
■ To consider an audience when making an argument.

# DESIGNING A PERSUASIVE LEAFLET
## WHAT YOU NEED
Paper, writing and drawing materials.

## WHAT TO DO
Remind the children of the leaflet they prepared for 'Wicked cars' (page 18). Tell them that they are now going to design an advertising leaflet for a new snack bar. First of all they need to come up with ideas for a delicious snack bar and give it a memorable, catchy name. Ask them to divide a sheet of paper into two columns. In one column, they can list all their ideas about the snack bar – what it contains (for example, nuts, chocolate, crispy flakes, fruit), what it tastes like, why people would want to buy it. In the other column, they should write down why snacking on sweet foods is not good for the teeth. Encourage the children to exchange information about tooth care and what happens when you eat sugary foods without cleaning your teeth afterwards. (Sugar sticks to the teeth, bacteria in the mouth react with it to make sticky plaque. This can make holes in tooth enamel and cause tooth decay.)

**OBJECTIVE**
■ To design a leaflet, making use of persuasive vocabulary and design features.

The children can then decide to either make a leaflet promoting the new snack bar or one that a dentist can use to persuade people not to snack on foods like this between meals because it will spoil their teeth.

Encourage the children to use the poster on photocopiable page 11 to remind them of features that can help in the construction of their leaflet. They may also want to use emphasis, exaggeration, different text sizes and diagrams to enhance and clarify their leaflets.

# State your case

Use this planner to structure a leaflet encouraging people to use their cars less and help to reduce global warming.

**Open with a statement that presents your case**

**Give a reason for the statement**

**Include facts and evidence**

**Summarise**

| | |
|---|---|
| Sea levels will rise. | We can all help by using our cars less. |
| Cars make greenhouse gases that cause global warming. | Air pollution in cities will get worse. |
| There will be more storms. | Cars are spoiling our planet. |
| Land will be flooded. | Global warming will cause many problems. |

# Good connections

Opinions need evidence to support them. Cut out all the statements, connectives and facts. Find two facts for each statement. Try to use different connective words to join the statements and facts. Then paste everything in place. Sometimes, you will need to put the fact *before* the statement.

**Statements**

Vegetarianism is good for the environment.

Vegetarianism can help to feed a hungry world.

A vegetarian diet is healthy.

**Choose a connective**

| because | so | as |
|---------|-----|-----|
| therefore | since | for example |

**Facts**

Plant crops use less water than animal farming.

Vegetarians have lower rates of some diseases than meat-eaters.

Clearing land for animal farming destroys the rainforest.

Famine could be reduced if the resources used to feed farm animals were used to feed people.

Vegetarian diets tend to be low in fat and high in fibre.

Rice and cereals are nutritious, and cheap to grow.

# Wicked cars

Some of these adjectives make sports cars sound good, some bad.
Circle the 'good' words in one colour and the 'bad' ones in another.
Then organise them into **for** or **against**. Write a few words to
explain what each adjective suggests about fast cars.

| | | | |
|---|---|---|---|
| sleek | dangerous | expensive | polluting |
| flashy | exciting | sporty | glamorous |

**For**

**Against**

*writing guides:* **PERSUASIVE WRITING**

# Try me

Can you help to sell these new products? Think of a catchy name and a memorable advertising slogan for each one.

**fruit drink**
- contains vitamin C
- gives you energy

**computer game**
- set in outer space
- action packed

**giant chips**
- extra large size
- oven or microwave cook

**comic or magazine**
- for 7- to 10-year-olds
- lots of sports features

# Vox pop

You are going to write a letter to a newspaper about computer games. Read these different views, then decide whether you support or oppose the games. Note down as many points as you can to support your argument.

Computer games are really exciting.

They can be harmful.

These games are very violent and they make the players violent.

They are expensive and a waste of money.

They can be educational.

They are great to play with friends.

You can get all sorts of skills from playing them.

They take up too much time.

Children turn into couch potatoes playing them.

You can get bored with them really quickly.

Continue on the back of the sheet if necessary…

# Points of view

Decide whether each of these statements is fact or opinion, and mark it with **F** or **O**. Note some evidence to support the facts, and explain why you agree or disagree with the opinions.

**Fact or opinion**

Smoking is bad for you.

Playing the lottery is a waste of money.

Cars cause pollution.

It is wrong to use animals in scientific experiments.

Exercise is good for you.

Watching television is a waste of time.

Mobile phones are just a nuisance.

# Be reasonable

You can use a persuasive text to convince one person or lots of people, but you need to think about who they are, and support your opinion with reasons. Add a topic of your own, then choose one to explain to your friend and one for the judges.

## Who are you persuading?

( Your friend )   ( A panel of judges )

## Persuade them that

| the best pop band is… | zoos should be banned | |
| more rubbish should be recycled | reading books is good for you | the best footballer is… |

I think _____

_____

_____

My reasons are
1. _____

_____

_____

2. _____

_____

_____

3. _____

_____

_____

I think _____

_____

_____

My reasons are
1. _____

_____

_____

2. _____

_____

_____

3. _____

_____

_____

*writing guides:* **PERSUASIVE WRITING**

*This section helps children to develop extended pieces of persuasive writing, using ideas explored in Sections One and Two. The activities support the children through developing and writing different forms of persuasive text.*

*Reference is made to the planning tasks completed in Sections One and Two, and the children will be able to make use of ideas and vocabulary generated by those tasks. It will be helpful for children to have access to the photocopiable sheets they completed for Section Two and the sample texts and poster from Section One.*

*Throughout this section, encourage the children to write their ideas in full sentences, and paragraphs where possible, using positive, persuasive language and a clear, logical structure.*

## Word appeal

Photocopiable page 25 helps children to focus on using strong, positive words and phrases, including exaggeration where appropriate. If possible, show the children some examples of estate agents' property details to familiarise them with the style of layout and wording. Explain that they need to read the facts that have been noted about the cottage and adapt them to make the place sound appealing – to persuade someone to buy it. Give them the context of describing the cottage for an information sheet that an estate agent could give to prospective buyers. Suggest to the children that they look back at the persuasive wording from 'Wicked cars' and 'Try me' (pages 18 and 19). They can use the spaces on the sheet to write short sentences based on and developing the notes given. They should then use a separate sheet of paper to set out their information in the style of an estate agent's property details.

## Save it!

In this activity, the children create a poster aiming to persuade people to save water. Start with a class discussion on why water is a precious resource: the world only has so much water, and when there are droughts there may not be enough to go around. When water is scarce, we must use it carefully. Can the children think of any ways of reducing how much we use? (For example, showering instead of having baths.)

Using A3 copies of photocopiable page 26, ask them first to think up a catchy heading for their poster, perhaps using alliteration. You might want to brainstorm a few ideas first. They can then write simple, snappy sentences inside the water drops to persuade people of the need to save water and ways of doing this (for example, turning the tap off when brushing teeth, having a rain butt in the garden.) Encourage the children to refer to the Oxfam appeal in Section One.

## Cars: a debate

Photocopiable page 27 helps the children to think up counter-arguments and set down reasons supporting them. It provides them with a framework to set out an argument against cars: are they the best or worst invention of the 20th century? Ask them to refer to the content on global warming, and the way they set out the evidence in 'State your case' in Section Two (page 16).

The sheet presents a speech in favour of cars for a debate on the motion 'Cars are the best invention of the 20th century'. The children can use the annotations given alongside the speech to help them with their counter-arguments putting the case against cars. Then ask them to write a short speech opposing the motion. They should refer to their work in Sections One and Two for methods on constructing a clear, credible argument that begins with a strong opening statement and closes with a convincing summary.

### After-school club

This writing frame on photocopiable page 28 helps the children to write a persuasive letter. Explain that they are going to write to some local firms asking them to sponsor an after-school sport and leisure club for their school. They need to persuade the sponsor that it will be worthwhile for them to fund the new club. Brainstorm ideas of activities and sports the children would like to see on offer, and how the club would benefit the pupils – helping them develop new skills, providing interest and a social setting for children who are bored or lonely, helping parents who work after school hours and so on. What equipment and space would they need? How would it benefit the sponsors? (For example, raising their profile in the local community, involving them in sports competitions and events.) Advise the children that thinking about the questions down the side of the writing frame will help to structure their letter and include the information they have brainstormed. Draw attention to the letter's hopeful conclusion.

### Meadow Vale

This activity, which will need at least two sessions, looks at a controversial planning issue from two points of view. Explain to the children that a new housing development is being proposed for a village. The developers want to build 50 new houses on a greenfield site on the edge of the village. Ask the children to imagine they work for the developer's marketing department and are writing brochures to persuade potential buyers that they are going to build modern houses in a lovely village setting. These new houses will be particularly suitable for young couples and families. Encourage the children to describe the facilities in the new homes (for example, garage, garden, fitted kitchen, dishwasher, washer-drier, power shower) and their pleasant village location and nearby amenities (such as village green, pub, school, shop, five miles from the railway station). You might want to list some of these ideas on the board.

Emphasise to the children that they need to think how the development can be described as a positive thing for the village – perhaps there is a shortage of good housing in the area; more young children in the area will encourage the authorities to keep the school open or mean it can have more funding.

The children can experiment with different ways of laying out their brochure, including gatefolds, appealing illustrations, bold headings, a brief introduction, bullet points and so on.

Now introduce the other side of the argument, using the pictures on photocopiable page 29. They represent different ways that the planned development will affect the village, its people, wildlife and environment. They indicate what will be lost if the greenfield site is built over and how the village may change for the worse. Tell the children to use the information in the pictures as evidence in a letter to the local planning authority opposing the development. Refer them to the letter against the wind farm at Scroby Sands in Section One and the 'State your case' plan in Section Two. Remind them to use powerful language, and connectives to link their statements with their evidence.

# Word appeal

Can you make this old cottage sound appealing? Write a positive sentence for each piece of information.

### Hundreds of years old

### Old thatched roof

### Steep stairs

### Tiny windows and doors

### Small rooms with low ceilings

### Lonely country location

### Big overgrown garden

### Needs a lot of work

# Save it!

Why do we need to save water?

How can we save water?

# Cars: a debate

**Monday 3 August 7.00pm**

*"Cars are the best invention of the 20th century."*

## Proposing the motion

- Cars have changed our lives more than any other invention in the 20th century.

- Journeys by car are fast and convenient.

- Cars help us get to school and work and do shopping.

- Cars let us visit friends and go on holiday.

- We feel safer travelling in cars than other modes of transport at night.

- Cars give us freedom and flexibility in travel.

- We need cars for the way we live today.

---

But how are cars changing the planet?

Wouldn't it be better to walk or cycle – better for us and the environment?

What about traffic jams?

What about road accidents?

Public transport is cheap and easy.

What about the noise and other pollution cars cause, and the environmental damage caused by road-building?

But what will happen if the number of cars on the roads goes on rising?

---

# After-school club

Write a letter to encourage sponsorship of an after-school sport and leisure club at your school.

Dear

Start by stating the purpose of the letter.

Why does the school need a club?

What will the club provide?

How will it help the pupils?

What will the sponsor get from it?

What help is needed?

We very much hope that you will want to be a part of our new club.

# Meadow Vale

Write a letter to oppose the housing development. Use these pictures of what will be lost to help you to explain *why* you think the development is a bad thing.

*writing guides:* **PERSUASIVE WRITING**

# SECTION FOUR
## REVIEW

*This review section helps children to identify strengths and weaknesses in their persuasive writing, and to evaluate examples of persuasive writing, good and bad. It also gives you an opportunity to appraise how well the children have understood and are using key features of the persuasive genre.*

*In assessing persuasive writing, it is helpful to play devil's advocate, challenging the children's statements and reasons with opposite points of view. This will encourage the children to think how to address and deal with counter-arguments, to make their writing more convincing.*

*As they review their work, remind the children of the generic features of persuasive writing (detailed throughout their work and on photocopiable page 11) and encourage them to relate their work to the activities they completed for Section Two.*

*Children can undertake the review activities individually, working with a writing partner or in groups.*

## Children's self-review

### Checkmate!
This sheet can be used for self-assessment or to assess writing with a partner or in small groups. It asks the children to read a persuasive text for the main points being made and think up arguments that put forward an opposite point of view. They should then look back at the text to see how effectively it addresses and dismisses each of their challenges. Encourage them to quote relevant words from the text, and if their counter-argument is not dealt with, suggest how it could be addressed. For example, if a persuasive text says *We need to build more motorways*, the children could challenge this with *Building more motorways will spoil the countryside*. They then look at the text to see if it addresses this argument. If not, they might suggest adding *However, the countryside must be protected when new motorways are planned*.

### Would you be persuaded?
The children can use this chart to review and edit their pieces of persuasive writing, or those written by their classmates. Ask them to check through their work to see if they can find good examples of generic features. If a feature is missing, or seems weak, they can try to improve their text by suggesting new sentences to be added or by revising existing ones.

## Other review methods

● Organise the children to work in pairs with a writing partner who plays devil's advocate and opposes their persuasive text with as many counter-arguments as they can. Stress that they are discussing an opinion, not criticising the text.
● Encourage the children to analyse examples of favourite advertisements and make notes on why they like them and think they are persuasive. Link this to 'branding' of clothes and other products, and what persuades us that we want to buy them. How do advertisers use persuasive images as well as words?
● Look at some health education leaflets on subjects such as smoking and drug taking. Discuss how persuasive the children find them and ask for suggestions on how they could be improved.